Documenting History

The Industrial
Revolution

Peter Hicks

WAYLAND

First published in 2009 by Wayland

Copyright © Wayland 2009

Wayland
338 Euston Road
London NW1 3BH

Wayland Australia
Level 17/207 Kent Street
Sydney, NSW 2000

Senior editor: Camilla Lloyd
Designer: Phipps Design
Consultant: Dr Andrew Dilley
Picture researcher: Shelley Noronha
Indexer and proof-reader: Cath Senker

Picture Acknowledgments: The author and publisher would like to thank the following for allowing their pictures to be reproduced in this publication: Cover: Main: Bettman/CORBIS, BL: Wolvertonhampton History & Heritage Society, BR: Wayland Picture Library; 1 Wayland Picture Library, 5 Mary Evans Picture Library, 6 Science Museum/Science &Society Picture Library, 8 Wolvertonhampton History & Heritage Society, 9 Guildhall Library, City of London,The Bridgeman Art Library,10 Public Record Office/HIP/Topfoto, 11 courtesy of the Ironbridge Gorge Museum Trust(www.ironbridge.org.uk <http://www.ironbridge.org.uk/>), 12 James Watt © Bettmann/CORBIS, 13 Wayland Picture Library, 14 Science Museum/Science & Society Picture Library, 15 Peter Hicks, 16 Science Museum, UK, London/The Bridgeman Art Library, 17,18 Peter Hicks, 19 Peter Newark American Collection/The Bridgeman Art Collection, 20 Mary Evans Picture Library, 21 Musee D'Orsay, Paris, France, Giraudon/The Bridgeman Art Library, 22 Peter Hicks, 23 Mary Evans Picture Library, 24 Wayland Picture Library, 25 National Railway Museum/Science and Society Picture Library, 27 Nationalgalerie, SMPK, Berlin, Germany/The Bridgeman Art Library, 28 Mary Evans Picture Library, 29 Science Museum/Science & Society Picture Library, 30 Currier and Ives/Getty Images, 32 Peter Newark American Pictures/The Bridgeman Art Library, 33 Peter Newark American Pictures/The Bridgeman Art Library, 34 Archives Charmet/The Bridgeman Art Library, 35 Akg-Images, 36 Mary Evans Picture Library, 37 Mary Evans Picture Library, 39 © Bettmann/CORBIS, 40 Guildhall Library, City of London/The Bridgeman Art Library, 41 Collection Kharbine-Tapabor, Paris, France/The Bridgeman Art Library, 42 Mary Evans Picture Library, 43 Hulton Archive/ Getty Images, 44 © Bettmann/CORBIS.

British Library Cataloguing in Publication Data:
    Hicks, Peter, 1952-
    The industrial revolution. - (Documenting history)
    1. Industrial revolution - Great Britain - Juvenile literature
    2. Industrial revolution - Great Britain - Sources - Juvenile literature
    I. Title
    941'.081

ISBN: 978 0 7502 5685 8

Printed in China

Wayland is a division of Hachette Children's Books, an Hachette UK company
www.hachettelivre.co.uk

CONTENTS

What was the Industrial Revolution?

The word 'revolution' means great change or upheaval. The upheaval that happened over many years in Britain during the 18th and 19th centuries was so remarkable that by 1851 Britain had become known as 'the workshop of the world'. Britain changed from a rural country, depending on the land and agriculture for its wealth, to the world's first industrial nation, where goods were manufactured in factories. These goods were then sold at home and abroad, encouraging trade and making the country wealthy. The Industrial Revolution that began in 18th - century Britain spread to Europe and the USA and changed the world.

Until around 1780, most Britons lived and worked on the land growing crops and rearing animals. Britain was a regional country, meaning that people lived and worked in their home villages or towns. Travel was very difficult because roads in most places were poor and transport was expensive, slow and uncomfortable. Each region had its own city or market town (where food and animals could be bought and sold) and a port allowing goods to be imported and exported by sea and river.

The population was small. In 1750 it was roughly 6 million and only one-fifth of people lived in towns. Over the next one hundred years the population tripled to about 20 million and by 1851 over half the people lived in towns and cities. Britain had transformed into an urban nation.

Britain did not depend only on agriculture before the industrial revolution. There were industries too – iron and textiles – but they were small scale. Woollen cloth was used for clothing and this was spun and weaved in people's cottages, often involving the whole family. This manual production was called the domestic system because it was centred on the home.

SOURCE

BOOK

'By all the processes being carried on under a man's roof, he retained his individual respectability; he was kept apart from associations that might injure his moral worth, whilst he generally earned wages which were sufficient to live comfortably upon …'

Peter Gaskell pointed out the advantages of the domestic system.

Peter Gaskell: extract from *The Manufacturing Population of England*, published in 1823.

Spinning on the green in Colchester, England. The scene in the painting looks idyllic, the domestic system was flexible and families could work when they had to.

Travelling merchants would deliver raw wool by packhorse and take away the woven cloth (yarn). Women spun the thread on their spinning wheels and men wove the cloth from the threads on their hand looms. There were shortages of thread because the invention of John Kay's 'flying shuttle' in 1733 had sped up the weaving process and allowed the weaver to produce wider cloth, which meant weaving was much faster than spinning. In one day, a weaver would use up the thread that had taken a spinner all week to produce.

Britain's small iron industry was also undeveloped. Although there were large deposits of iron ore in Britain, there was a serious lack of fuel to smelt it. Until the early 18th century charcoal was used as the main fuel, but the woodlands providing the trees for the charcoal were being used up. Some iron was imported instead from Sweden, Germany and Russia where there were huge wood reserves.

The rapid population growth between 1700 and 1900 changed Britain and quickened the transition from manual production at home to machine production in factories. Britain's industrial changes aroused interest in Europe and the USA. It would not remain workshop of the world for very long.

The importance of population and agriculture

During the 18th century agriculture went through a revolution that transformed the look of the British countryside. The cause of this change was primarily population growth. Between 1700 and 1800, Britain's population increased by 3.5 million to about 10 million. There were many more mouths to feed and this put huge demands on food production. As demand increased, the price of food went up. This in turn created an incentive for enterprising farmers to make healthy profits from their land.

To achieve this, farmers had to modernize their traditional systems of agriculture. The open-field system that dated from the Middle Ages, with its small strips of land dotted around a village, could produce enough food when the population was small. When the population increased dramatically this old system could not cope. The old system was not very efficient. For example, at any one time, one-third of the land was fallow; it was not farmed in order to allow the soil to regain its nutrients.

SOURCE

BOOK

'...by nineteen out of twenty enclosure bills, the poor are injured, and some grossly injured.'

The agricultural writer, Arthur Young, admitted that enclosure caused a great deal of hardship to many.

Arthur Young in *Reformation to Industrial Revolution* by Christopher Hill, 1967.

A model of S. Morton's seed drill, 1828. The drill sowed seeds at an even rate per yard and could be adjusted to vary the depth, according to the farmer's requirements.

Rich farmers bought up many of the strips of land and enclosed them into larger fields. To do this, farmers had to get an Enclosure Act passed through Parliament. As Parliament at that time represented the landowners, this was easily passed. Nearly 5,000 acts were passed between 1761 and 1800.

Once the bigger farmers put ditches and hedges in the fields on their neat farms, they could improve the soil and experiment with new crops, animal breeds and machinery.

A new four-year crop rotation replaced the old and wasteful three-year cycle of wheat, barley and fallow. Farmers now planted wheat, turnips, barley (or oats) and clover. This put land under cultivation all the time, with the turnips and clover replacing nitrogen in the soil.

Under the old system, animals often became ill by mixing together on the common land. The new hedged fields allowed for the introduction of new breeds of stronger, heavier animals.

Previously, seed was scattered onto the soil in the 'broadcast' method and this was very wasteful. New machines such as the seed drill increased the yields of crops while using less seed. With the revolution in agriculture underway, people received a more plentiful and varied diet. Not surprisingly, this helped the population to increase as it became healthier. An increase in population was important for two reasons. Firstly,

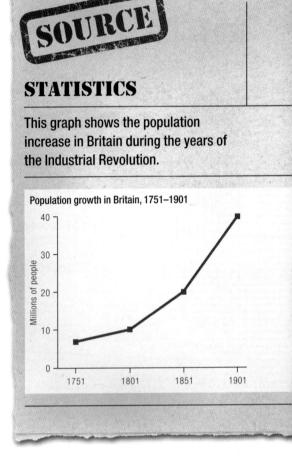

SOURCE

STATISTICS

This graph shows the population increase in Britain during the years of the Industrial Revolution.

Population growth in Britain, 1751–1901

there was a bigger workforce to work in the mills, factories and workshops. Secondly, this workforce would have to buy goods and services such as clothes, shoes, housing and food. This demand gave a huge boost to industry and agriculture.

Another result of the agricultural revolution was the drift of people from the countryside to the towns. Small farmers sold their strips of land and after spending the money they had made, tried their luck in the new and expanding towns and cities.

7

Paying for the Industrial Revolution

In the late 18th century Britain was booming. A whole infrastructure of roads, canals, mills, docks and warehouses was created. Where did all the money to pay for this come from? A great deal of the funding came from abroad. Britain was building up an empire and colonies such as India were very valuable. The East India Company pioneered trade in India, especially in textiles, and fortunes were made, much of it returning to Britain.

During this time slaves from Africa were bought with British exports and then traded in the Caribbean and the USA in return for raw materials. Huge profits were amassed from the slave trade. Enormous personal fortunes were made from slavery by businessmen dealing in ships, tobacco, cotton, sugar and rum. Much of these profits were then poured into economic ventures at home. The slave trade relied on selling goods, often cotton imported from India. This market was one that industrialists were later able to exploit. The ports of Bristol and Liverpool engaged in the slave trade and were then able to invest in new docks and warehouses.

SOURCE

SHARE CERTIFICATE

The share certificate is for one share in the Darlaston Steel and Iron Company Limited. Richard Bills formed the company in 1826 and by the 1850s the site of the furnaces and foundry covered over 55 acres. The company eventually employed about 2,000 people and on Bills' stepson's retirement was sold to the Lloyd family for a quarter of a million pounds. This share certificate dates from October 1875.

The Bank of England, Threadneedle Street, London. Founded in 1694, it looked after the government's accounts and provided loans in peace and wartime.

Some money came into Britain from other nations such as the Netherlands, which saw Britain as a safe and profitable country in which to invest. However, a huge amount of the investment for the Industrial Revolution came from British landowners and farmers at home, who were making substantial profits from their modern farms and estates. They placed their savings in the hundreds of new banks that sprang up after 1780. These banks would then lend money to businessmen starting new enterprises, such as cotton production. By 1800 there was a huge amount of money in circulation. There were 400 private banks around the country – often based in market towns – and 70 banks in London alone.

These banks did not only provide loans, but also allowed bills to be paid. Banks started introducing cheques, which allowed businessmen to settle transactions without having to move large amounts of cash around. If someone had an idea for a new business project they did not have to go to a bank for a loan. They could form a company and issue shares in it. If people bought shares they became shareholders in the company. If the company was a success, they would receive a share of the profits.

An example of such a project was the Ironbridge – the world's first bridge made of iron – built across the River Severn near Coalbrookdale in Shropshire. To pay for it the company issued 64 shares priced at £50 each. This was a very high price at that time. When all the shares were sold, the money paid for the design, materials and labour to build the bridge. It opened in 1781, and users were charged a toll (fee) to cross it. From these tolls, the shareholders received a share of the profits. Many enjoyed a good return on their initial investment.

The importance of inventions and entrepreneurs

Another reason the Industrial Revolution happened first in Britain was the appearance of important inventions at critical times. We have seen that the speed of spinning lagged behind that of weaving. In 1765 James Hargreave's Spinning Jenny (named after his wife) was the first step in the advance in spinning. The first machine made in Blackburn, Lancashire had eight spindles harnessed to a hand treadle (a lever used to turn a wheel). As the machines developed further the number of spindles increased to 80. By 1788 there were 20,000 machines in operation (small ones in cottages and large ones in factories). A disadvantage of the jenny was that although it spun good weft (the cross thread), it did not spin good warp (the long thread).

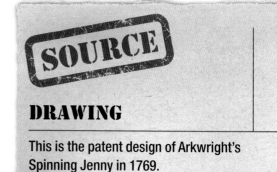

SOURCE

DRAWING

This is the patent design of Arkwright's Spinning Jenny in 1769.

This particular problem was solved by Richard Arkwright, from Preston, Lancashire, one of the great pioneer businessmen of the Industrial Revolution. The machine he invented was the Water Frame consisting of rollers and spindles that stretched the thread and made it strong enough for both warp and weft. As its name suggests, it was powered by water and not suitable for use in the home. In 1771, Arkwright built a factory to produce cotton cloth in Cromford, Derbyshire, powered by the fast-flowing river Derwent.

Arkwright was a dynamic entrepreneur, or 'risk taker' who was constantly looking to make money by providing people with goods they wanted. When unemployed and disgruntled spinners burnt down one of his mills, he simply opened another one. He died in 1782, one of the richest men in Britain.

One disadvantage of the Water Frame was that the yarn produced was strong but coarse. This meant the yarn could not be made into high-quality cotton fabric. Samuel Crompton, a weaver from Bolton, Lancashire devised a machine that produced yarn that was strong and fine. In 1779, he crossed the Spinning Jenny with the Water Frame, creating a machine known as the Mule (a mule is a cross between a donkey and a horse). Once perfected, spinning was revolutionized and by 1812 Mules drove millions of

William Reynolds was a businessman and an inventor who built a canal network linking his ironworks, mines and factories in Shropshire. Two of his canals were on different levels, so he built a huge lift (Britain's first inclined plane) at Ketley Bank to raise the barges between them.

spindles all over northern Britain. The textile industry was firmly based in large factories, powered by fast-flowing rivers and streams. Richard Arkwright was one of many entrepreneurs who prospered during these years. Successful entrepreneurs understood that new goods needed to be in demand. They also realized that a knowledge of science and technology would benefit them. They understood the importance of investment and that cheap transport of raw materials and finished products was crucial.

Steam

Before the Industrial Revolution, wind, horses and water provided power. These sources were unreliable – the wind did not always blow, in the summer rivers and streams could dry up, and horse power was expensive. There was always a demand for power so people started experimenting to find a source of power that was constant, cheap and not dependent on the weather.

The breakthrough came from solving the problem of flooding in tin, copper and coal mines. Thomas Savery, a military engineer from Cornwall,

James Watt in his laboratory working on a model of a Newcomen engine. It was after he successfully mended it that he improved the engine's design.

where there were many tin mines, developed his so-called 'Miner's Friend' in 1698. It was a pump designed to raise water from flooded mines, but proved to be too slow and expensive.

Ten years later, Thomas Newcomen, a locksmith from Dartmouth in Devon, developed the first successful fire-driven machine. It consisted of a cylinder pushing up a piston attached to a crossbeam. When the steam drove up the piston, cold water was sprayed into the cylinder to make it drop down again. At the other end of the beam a rod pumped water from the mine. Again, this engine was very expensive because the cooling system used so much fuel. Also its action, a beam moving up and down, meant that it could pump up and down but couldn't turn a wheel. This limited what the engine could do. However, by the mid-18th century it still proved popular in mines all over the country.

Two important developments were to make steam engines more attractive. In 1764, James Watt, a brilliant maker of scientific instruments, mended a Newcomen engine. In doing so he radically improved its performance by overcoming its weaknesses. Instead of cooling the hot cylinder, Watt designed the cooling to take place in a separate condenser connected to the cylinder. The condenser could be kept cool while the cylinder was hot. Huge savings on fuel were made. Watt patented his engine with a separate condenser in 1769. Cheap and efficient steam power was now a possibility.

Later in 1781, Watt discovered that if he attached a rod to the crossbeam and placed a small cog rotating around a bigger one – the 'Sun and Planet' gears – it could drive wheels. This rotary motion could power the new spinning machines in the cotton mills that were previously powered by water. The engines were also used in ironworks, coal and tin mines, on canals for raising barges and pumping water and in breweries, brick works and china factories. With more and more steam engines in use, there was a massive demand for coal. Industries sprung up

ENGINE PLAN

This plan shows James Watt's double-action Sun and Planet gears engine drawn in 1788.

JAMES WATT 1788
DOUBLE-ACTION SUN-AND-PLANET ENGINE

on and near the coalfields of the Midlands and in northern Britain, Scotland and South Wales so they could be near the fuel that powered the engines. James Watt's partner, the entrepreneur Matthew Boulton who helped build 1,200 Boulton and Watt engines by 1800 boasted; *'I sell, sir, what all the world desires – power'*.

The importance of coal

In the early 18th century the coal industry was undeveloped and produced only 2 million tonnes a year. Much of this was used as domestic fuel although some was exported to Europe. Most of this coal was mined near Newcastle and transported by ships mainly to London and ports along the south and east coasts.

The coal industry was small scale because mining technology was still primitive. Coal was mined when it was near the surface. Mining deeper seams was dangerous and expensive. Flooding was a serious problem, and so too were poor ventilation and potential explosions and cave-ins. Another difficulty was getting the coal to the surface.

SOURCE

PARLIAMENTARY PAPERS

'The youngest children in the mines ... are called ... trappers ... it is a most ... dull dungeon-like life these little creatures are doomed to spend; a life, for the most part, passed in the solitude, damp and darkness.'

Extract from *Children's Employment Commission (Mines), Parliamentary Papers*, 1842, Vol. XVI.

Pit explosions were depressingly common in the 18th and 19th centuries. Thousands of mine workers were killed in explosions before the compulsory inspection of pits was introduced in 1850. At first, seven inspectors were responsible for the safety of 3,000 mines.

With the increasing popularity of steam engines there was a huge demand for coal as fuel. Mine owners were encouraged to dig deeper and bigger mines. This led to a build up of poisonous and explosive gases, making safe ventilation essential. Miners had their own names for these killer gases. Carbonic acid gas was named 'chokedamp'. It couldn't be seen but a tell-tale sign of its presence was when a miner's candle was put out. Methane gas is highly explosive and was known as 'firedamp'. This was visible and it was said it *'lay like snow in a drift'.*

The early system of ventilation consisted of digging shafts on different levels which allowed air to be drawn from one and up the other. To increase the air flow, a furnace was placed at the bottom of the up-shaft of the mine, drawing more clean air in. By the early 19th century pumps were being used and ventilation slowly improved, but the death rate from explosions was high.

A big threat came from explosions caused by the use of naked flames in the pit. There were only two possible forms of lighting – candles and steel spark mills – and both could be lethal. The Davy Lamp and the Stephenson Lamp were invented in 1816. These lamps encouraged pit owners to send miners into even deeper and more dangerous places. In 1866, 651 miners were killed in firedamp explosions. Owing to the huge demand for coal,

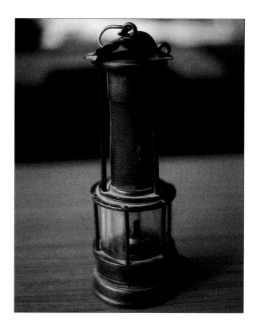

The strip of wire gauze around the Davy Lamp that surrounded the flame conducted away its heat and prevented it from lighting any gas present.

there was a shortage of labour in the mines. Women and children were employed in shocking conditions. Women carried baskets of coal up flights of steps to the surface. Young girls pulled trucks of coal with chain ropes around their waists.

In this haphazard way, coal production increased. In 1770, 6 million tonnes were produced, rising to 10 million in 1800. By 1820 this doubled to an impressive 20 million tonnes. It was not just steam engines that consumed vast amounts of coal. The iron industry also started to demand coal after Abraham Darby, an iron master, discovered a way of smelting (extracting the metal from its ore) iron ore by using coal.

The iron masters

Britain's wood supplies for smelting iron ore were running so low that many iron masters tried to find a replacement for charcoal. They experimented with coal but the impurities in it produced brittle and unworkable iron.

In 1709, Abraham Darby found that by reducing coal to coke – the sulphur was burnt away – he could smelt the iron ore into good pig iron, which was brittle but good for casting into cannon, pillars and pots. Coke-smelted pig iron could not be heated and beaten into wrought iron because it crumbled when hammered. The use of coke spread very slowly – it was a Darby family secret until the 1750s – and in 1760 there were only 17 coke furnaces in the whole of Britain.

It was said that Abraham Darby II first converted coke-produced pig iron into wrought iron, but he didn't leave any records. The man who patented it in 1784 was Henry Cort, working at Fontly Forge in Hampshire. He smelted the iron ore in a special furnace that used coal. The heat from the coal was reflected onto the iron ore by a specially angled furnace roof so

SOURCE

PAINTING

This dramatic painting by P. J. de Loutherbourg (1808) shows the powerful iron furnaces of Coalbrookdale, Shropshire, blasting out fire and heat.

that impurities did not spoil the iron. When the iron became molten, it was 'puddled', or stirred with iron hooks, which allowed the carbon to burn off, leaving iron that could be shaped. In fact, Cort had invented a 'rolling-mill'. The metal passed between grooved rollers, making bars of iron. It was much quicker than the old method of heating and hammering by hand. Darby had improved the speed of pig iron production and Cort had perfected the turning of it into wrought iron. All this required coal, which Britain had in plentiful supply. Britain was entering a new 'iron age'.

Perhaps the greatest iron master of the age was John Wilkinson, nicknamed 'Iron Mad' Wilkinson. Based in Birmingham, though he had works in Coalbrookdale, his father had been one of the first iron ore smelters to adopt Darby's coke method. He

The Ironbridge in Shropshire, England. The world's first iron bridge, it was completed in 1779 at a cost of over £3,000. The bridge contains 378 tons of cast iron.

himself had been an early purchaser of a Boulton-Watt steam engine. The iron output was enormous. His ironworks helped to build the world's first iron bridge near Coalbrookdale in association with Abraham Darby III.

Wilkinson provided the city of Paris with 40 miles of iron pipes for its water system. In 1787 he successfully launched the first river barge on the River Severn made from an iron plate. When Britain fought Napoleon in Spain – the Peninsular War (1808–14) – most of the cannon were made by Wilkinson. It was his skill in casting cannon that allowed engineers like James Watt to produce precise cylinders in their steam engines. Wilkinson died in 1808 and was buried in an iron coffin.

How factories worked

The new water – and later steam-driven mills – or factories that were built in the later 18th century were far more efficient than the old domestic system of industry. The machines and workforce were all in one place and everybody inside the factory buildings had a particular job to do.

In his book *The Wealth of Nations* (1776) the Scottish economist Adam Smith showed how a greater *'increase in the quantity of work'* resulted from the *'division of labour'*. He then showed how 16 different operations and

workers could successfully manufacture pins. This division of labour was applied to the cotton industry.

The cotton mills had many floors with employees working on one part of the production process. In the Lancashire mills this involved washing the raw cotton first, then carding (combing) it into strands ready to spin them on the water frames or mules into yarn ready for weaving. The jobs in these processes were varied. Reelers, winders and frame cleaners all required different skills. Children were employed to change the bobbins and mend snapped threads.

A cotton mill in full operation. Note the young girl cleaning the machinery while it is still moving. Mills like this were extremely noisy, hot, dusty and dangerous.

Power looms were not in full use until the 1830s so the weaving – especially for fancy cloths – was still performed by hand-loom weavers. With so much work the weavers were in great demand and it was said you could tell a weaver in a northern town *'by the £5 notes in his hat-band'*.

Power was transmitted to all floors and processes by a series of gears, shafts and belts connected to either a water wheel or steam engine. The factory buildings themselves had to be strong to cope with the weight of the machines and their continual violent motions. The first mills were made of wood and stone, but after a series of disastrous fires, cast iron columns, beams and joists replaced wood in the 1790s.

Cotton production was centred on Lancashire for a number of important reasons. The soft water and damp climate helped the spinning. The presence of the Lancashire coalfields assisted expansion when steam power replaced water. Vast amounts of raw cotton grown on the slave plantations in the southern states of the USA were imported through the port of Liverpool. The volume of exports increased after the development of Eli Whitney's 'cotton gin' (short for

ENGRAVING

The cotton gin, invented by Eli Whitney in 1793, increased the demand for slaves in cotton production. This engraving shows their part in the process.

'engine')in 1793. First, circular saws removed the fibre from the seeds and then the fibre was removed by a revolving brush. This significantly sped up the process. In 1792, the USA exported 295 bales of cotton rising to 36,000 bales in 1800. By the 1840s, 85% of cotton spun in British mills came from the southern states of the USA. There was a constant demand for cotton clothing by the working class in the 19th century because it was cheap, light and easy to wash.

Working conditions

In time the new machines that transformed cotton production would spread to the woollen industry. Yorkshire woollen production prospered because the mills were close to coalfields, which provided a ready supply of fuel. For this reason, the East Anglia and Somerset woollen industries went into decline. By the early 19th century there were over half a million people working in the textile industry. What were conditions like?

The workers found the discipline of factory life very hard. Time keeping was vital. Clocks, bells and whistles dictated their shifts – the amount of time they had to work. This was a world away from the old domestic system under which people worked when they needed to.

The mills were noisy, dusty, unbearably hot in the summer and lit by gas lamps in the winter. Many machine operators worked very long

Campaigners like Richard Oastler were very concerned about the treatment of children in mills and factories. He likened their conditions to those of the slaves in the southern states of the USA.

FACTORY FINES

Any spinner found with his window open	1s (5p)
Any spinner found washing himself	1s (5p)
Any spinner putting his gas out too soon	1s (5p)
Any spinner found whistling	1s (5p)
Any spinner being five minutes late after the last bell rings	2s (10p)

The factory fines above were just some of the harsh rules enforced in many mills. If spinners broke the rules they had to pay the fines from their wages.

Fines from William Cobbett's *Political Register, Vol. II*, 20 November 1824.

shifts, often 15 to 16 hours a day. A combination of the long hours and early starts (5 or 6 in the morning) led to tiredness and accidents. There were many examples of workers dragged into unfenced machinery by their clothes or hair causing dreadful mutilation.

The men in charge of the machines –'overseers' – were very strict and workers could be fined for breaking the rules. If a spinner arrived five minutes after the shift bell rang he or she was fined 2 shillings (10p). This was a serious deduction from a weekly wage packet of between 50p and £1.

The work was hardest for the large numbers of children employed in the factories. These noisy places scared and bewildered the very young. Small children were popular with factory owners because they were cheap to employ and could clean the machinery while it was still running.

Why did parents allow their children to carry out this dangerous and tiring work? Many parents were poor and needed more money to come into the home. Other children were orphans sent from workhouses and orphanages to work as apprentices in the factories. Some of these children were treated very badly.

Not all factory owners were cruel. Robert Owen's New Lanark mill in upper Clydesdale, Scotland, provided a model village, school, places of worship and good working conditions for his workers. Men did not work more than ten and a half hours a day and children under the age of ten did not work.

Metal workers in a foundry, 1893. Owing to unpleasant conditions – intense heat, smoke and the dangers of molten iron – injuries were common.

Manufacturing did not just take place in the cotton and woollen mills of the Midlands and northern Britain. The Industrial Revolution created demand for a whole range of products that were produced in workshops (small factories), forges, brickyards and sweatshops in all the big towns and cities. Men, women and children toiled in overcrowded, poorly ventilated and often harmful conditions to produce the iron, ropes, bricks, nails, chains and glass that industrialization demanded.

Roads and canals

Britain would never have been able to industrialize without a revolution in transport. We know Britain was very regional before the 1780s, and if industry and business were to thrive, communications needed to improve.

At the start of the 18th century, roads in Britain were poor. Little better than tracks, they became impassable in winter. River transport was limited because in the summer, water levels dropped so low that rivers were hard for barges and ships to navigate.

After the 1750s, roads started to improve because of the impact of Turnpike Trusts. A Trust consisted of businessmen who raised money and got permission through an Act of Parliament to build or improve a road. Then they charged travellers tolls to use it. Toll houses with gates were built at each end of the road and the toll money was used to maintain the road and improve other roads.

The Trusts employed great road engineers such as Thomas Telford (1757–1834), whose London to Holyhead road contained the spectacular suspension bridge that linked Wales with the island of Anglesey. John McAdam (1756–1836) perfected a raised, cambered (curved) road surface made of layers of stone, with drainage ditches on either side. The weight of the traffic compressed the stones to form a 'macadam' surface.

The turnpike network improved journey times – mail and ideas travelled quickly – and business communications improved. In the mid-18th century a horse-drawn coach journey between Edinburgh and London took between 8 and 10 days.

TABLE OF TOLLS

This was a list of the toll payments required to cross the Ironbridge in Shropshire.

By 1836 this had been reduced to roughly 45 hours. Mail coaches began in 1784 and by 1800 almost 400 towns were getting a daily post delivered by coaches that could travel on average 6 miles per hour. However, industrial processes involved bulky goods – coal or iron ore – and sending these goods by road was difficult and expensive.

The Duke of Bridgewater, a coal mine owner in Worsley, found that the cost of sending his coal by packhorse to

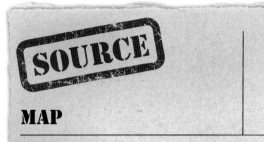

SOURCE

MAP

This is a map showing the route of a proposed canal from Worsley to Manchester and then to the Mersey by the engineer James Brindley for the Duke of Bridgewater.

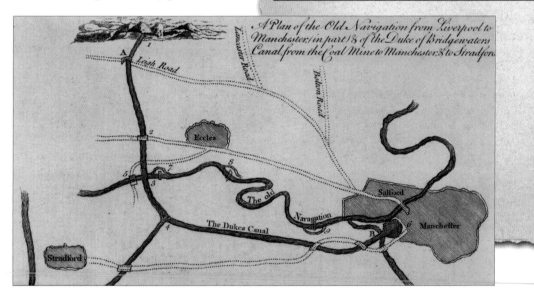

A Plan of the Old Navigation from Liverpool to Manchester; in part 8 of the Duke of Bridgewaters Canal from the Coal Mine to Manchester; 8 to Stradfor

Manchester, 8 miles away, was unprofitable. He decided to build a canal instead and hired a millwright, James Brindley, to design it. In 1759 and 1760 Parliament passed the acts allowing construction to begin. The impressive canal contained an aqueduct over the River Irwell and two tunnels, one of which had a water-driven crane that lifted the tubs of coal up a vertical shaft to the surface. The construction nearly bankrupted the duke, but with an income of £3 million a year, he soon got his investment back. The Grand Trunk Canal, linking the rivers Trent and Mersey, opened in 1777 and travelled through five tunnels and over five aqueducts. Over the next 70 years a 4,000-mile network of canals was made, linking up all the coalfields, industrial towns, cities and important rivers.

Railway Mania

Although the canals helped to revolutionize transport in the early 19th century they were still not perfect forms of transit. Journey times were slow because of the many locks that barges had to go through when canals climbed hills. Canal docks became very congested, and goods could be held up for many weeks. Gradually, canal owners increased their prices, so businessmen were keen to try alternative methods of carriage.

The railway, or 'tramway' to use its original name, was an old idea and had been used in mines and quarries where animals pulled wagons full of coal or stone. Some engineers experimented with steam locomotion. In 1805, Richard Trevithick's Catch Me Who Can entertained paying passengers on a circular demonstration track in London. The attraction proved popular but businessmen were uninterested in investing in it. In 1812 William Hedley, a manager of a colliery in Northumberland designed the Puffing Billy, another early steam locomotive. However, it was George Stephenson, a colliery engine maker – known later as the 'father of the railways' – who made an impression on the owners of the proposed Stockton to Darlington railway.

On 27 September 1825, Stephenson's engine Locomotion pulling wagons loaded with coal and, flour (and about 600 people), arrived in Stockton. The railway age had begun. Stephenson and his son Robert designed the Rocket that opened the Liverpool and Manchester railway in September 1830. The businessmen who had the foresight to invest in this project saved £20,000 in transport costs in six months. Railways could make money out of carrying goods and passengers.

There followed a period of expansion called Railway Mania. The success of the Stockton to Darlington and Liverpool to Manchester railways encouraged others to invest in the railways. There was money in Britain ready to be invested that had come from other successes of the Industrial

The excited spectators follow and cheer Stephenson's Locomotion at the opening of the Stockton to Darlington railway in 1825.

Revolution, such as the textile industry. By 1851, nearly 7,000 miles of track had been laid and it took over from the canal network in linking up the major centres of population, business and industry in Britain.

A huge army of navigators ('navvies') had built, largely by hand, an impressive infrastructure of cuttings, embankments, bridges, tunnels and viaducts that carried the tracks. Their achievement, which cost the lives of many navvies, can be seen today. Railway construction boosted British industries. There was huge demand for iron, coal, bricks, timber, gravel and steam engines.

The railways created a boom in Britain. People were employed to build and run them. The speedy transit of raw materials and goods brought down costs and opened up new markets. Farmers for example, could send their perishable produce (such as milk) to nearby cities by train, improving their income and the population's diet.

RAILWAY MAP

This is George Bradshaw's map of the British railway network in 1851. Bradshaw was originally a map maker for canals and railways. In 1839, he began to publish railway timetables.

Europe follows Britain

Britain's success as the world's first industrial nation aroused the interest of its neighbours in Europe. Numerous groups of businessmen visited Britain in the 1820s and 1830s and were undoubtedly impressed by the mills, factories, forges and mines that were powered by the smoke-belching steam engines. Many, it must be said, were also horrified by the filth, squalor and pollution they noticed in the industrial areas and where the workers lived.

Spurred on by Britain's lead and the desire to modernize and make money, the Industrial Revolution spread east and south across Europe after 1820. The pace of change was not the same in every country. In some areas, towns that were on or near a coalfield changed and developed quickly. Northern France and the Ruhr valley in Germany adopted new mining and metal-working techniques quickly. Other parts of France, where there were huge timber reserves, were still using charcoal to smelt iron ore. In fact as late as 1848, half of France's iron still came from charcoal furnaces.

Some countries with good reserves of raw materials lacked transport structures. This is why Russia and Germany had to invest in railways first to allow industrialization to follow. British locomotives were used in these country's early railways.

After Britain, the next country to industrialize was France in about 1820, but slow population growth held it back. Germany started the process in 1840 and was an established industrial power by 1900, leading the world in some branches of chemical production, notably synthetic dyestuffs. Sweden, with huge reserves of iron ore, began industrializing in 1850. Austria, Italy

SOURCE

BOOK

'A sort of black smoke covers the city. The sun seen through it is a disc without rays. Under this half-daylight 300,000 human beings are ceaselessly at work. A thousand noises disturb this dark, damp labyrinth, but they are not at all the ordinary sounds one hears in great cities.'

Alexis de Tocqueville was a French political thinker. He was shocked by what he saw in the city of Manchester when he travelled there in the 19th century.

Alexis de Tocqueville in *Journeys from England and Ireland*, 1835.

A German ironworks in Berlin, 1875. Metalworking was crucially important to Germany's industrialization. In 1850 it employed 12% of the manufacturing workforce. Fifty years later this had risen to 27%.

and northern Spain began the process in 1870, and Russia the latest, in 1890. Russia, although potentially very powerful, was hampered by a lack of finance to invest in industry. By 1914 nearly half of Russia's capital for industry had come from abroad. Most of Europe was undergoing some measure of industrial transformation in 1900, with the exception of theBalkans.

Another factor determining the pace of industrialization was political stability. Some countries were very stable in the 19th century, others less so. Between 1789 and 1871, France went through four revolutions and lost two major wars. Russia was involved in two unsuccessful wars against Britain and France in 1854 and Japan in 1904–5. It also experienced a serious revolution in 1905. Germany on the other hand became a united country

after Prussia (the most powerful German state) waged two successful wars against Austria in 1866 and France in 1870–71. Germany's success in these wars boosted industry.

Britain was fortunate that there were no massive political upheavals at home in the 19th century. It was evolving into a reasonably stable democracy. After its success in the Napoleonic wars, which led to an increase in iron production, Britain did not fight another war in Europe until World War I in 1914. There is no doubt that Britain's industrial success inspired business leaders and governments across Europe to copy developments in textiles, coal mining and heavy industry.

27

The USA industrializes

In 1800 the USA was a modest agricultural country, 83% per cent of its workforce worked on the land. Its population was only 4 to 5 million. Over the next 60 years the USA was to undergo a dramatic transformation. Its population rose to 30 million and the number of people living in towns and cities tripled. In 1860, the USA had 9 cities with over 100,000 people in each (Britain had 7). The New York–Brooklyn conurbation exceeded a million inhabitants and the city of Philadelphia, half a million. This represented a huge market for home- produced goods. The expansion came about because the northern states of the USA underwent their own revolution in industry.

How did this revolution start? As in Britain, textiles were very important. Many countries looked to Britain for technology and expertise. The USA was no exception, and merchants from New England sent a group to Britain to recruit skilled workers. The British government responded by passing a law forbidding new plans, machines or skilled labour from leaving the country.

However, in 1789, Samuel Slater (1768–1835), the manager of a Lancashire mill, secretly emigrated to the USA with the plans of all the

Robert Fulton's **Clermont** *on the Hudson River between New York and Albany. The 'Watt-type' engine burnt pine wood and was described as a* **'monster moving on the waters ... breathing flames and smoke.'**

own. By 1800, 2,000 spindles were working, but by 1815, stimulated by the war against Britain in 1812, there were 130,000 spindles operating in more than 200 mills. When Slater died in 1835 (a very rich man) he had set up mills in Rhode Island, Massachusetts, New Hampshire and Connecticut.

By 1825, the UK parliament had lifted the export ban. Many textile workers were encouraged to move to the USA with their machines and know-how. Lowell, a town in Massachusetts, was founded at this time by Boston merchants on the Merrimac River, a good source of power for the new mills. It was soon a thriving settlement, and power looms for weaving were introduced, based on the latest British designs. Similar towns were founded along the Merrimac and in southern Maine.

US engineers did not always get their ideas from abroad. From the 1790s many inventions were successfully developed at home. In 1795 Oliver Evans designed an automated flour mill. Eli Whitney, having won the contract to produce 10,000 rifles for the government in 1800, perfected their assembly with interchangeable parts. In 1793, Robert Fulton, an engineer, began designing his paddle steamer, emerging as the *Clermont* in 1807. US industry was steadily developing.

The 'father of American industry', Samuel Slater. His expertise and extraordinary drive gave the US textile industry a huge boost.

important spinning machinery in his head. Employed by two merchants called William Almy and Moses Brown in Rhode Island, he discarded their old machinery and with the help of a local carpenter who was sworn to secrecy, he started making a Water Frame. In December 1790, production began in the USA's first water-driven spinning mill at Pawtucket, Rhode Island.

The factory made a good profit from the start, and Slater soon set up on his

The USA advances

With business taking off in the early 19th century, the USA had to improve its transport links. The cost of transit was very high and this rose with the building of turnpike roads that charged for travel. Steamboats appeared on rivers, the Great Lakes and along the coast, assisting trade. Probably the most impressive engineering project at this time was the Erie Canal. It took nine years to construct, was 364 miles long and linked up the Atlantic Ocean with the

The New York and Erie Railroad at Hornellsville, an important junction for travellers to Cleveland or Buffalo. Its owners claimed it was **'the most direct route from New York to all Western cities and towns.'**

Great Lakes. By lowering transport costs by 90% it provided a massive boost to industry.

Once again, all these projects needed finance. Where did it come from? In 1800 there were only 28 banks in the whole of the USA, but by 1818 the number had risen to 300, with deposits of $160 million in total. The banks and insurance companies encouraged people to save. This, along with profits from agriculture and the successful textile industry, all increased bank deposits. These funds were lent out to entrepreneurs, who invested in factories or civil engineering projects.

US industrialists adopted machines much more quickly than the British did. This was because there was a shortage of skilled labour. Factory owners invested in complex machines that could be operated by unskilled workers. A good example was the sewing machine patented by Elias Howe in 1846. It rapidly created a 'ready-made' clothing industry and could be adapted for use in the shoe industry.

The USA was fortunate in having Pennsylvania – a state rich in iron ore and coal that became the centre of the USA's heavy industry. The first blast furnace was established by Scottish immigrants, and Andrew Carnegie, also a Scottish immigrant, introduced the Bessemer process for converting iron into steel in 1868.

The shortage of skilled labour in the 1830s and 1840s was overcome by the arrival of European immigrants from countries such as Germany, Sweden, England, Scotland and Wales. Thousands of people fled the Irish potato famine and emigrated too.

The USA rapidly expanded westwards during the 1830s at the expense of many Native Americans. Farmers settled the land in very difficult circumstances – it took $600 to establish a farm in Ohio or Indiana. The lack of population and labourers meant that farmers, like factory owners, had to use the latest machinery and cultivation techniques if they were

NEWSPAPER

'…our manifest destiny to overspread the continent allotted [sic] by Providence for the free development of your yearly multiplying millions.'

John L. O'Sullivan, editor of the *Democratic Review*, justified the USA's drive west that would lead to the violent confiscation of land from the Native Americans.

John L. O'Sullivan in the *Democratic Review*, July 1845.

to survive. Survive they mostly did. Cities and towns developed. Chicago, fast approaching 100,000 inhabitants in the 1850s, was the centre of farm machinery production. Railway construction tripled during the 1850s. The cities of the 'new West' – La Crosse, St Louis and Chicago – were all linked by rail to the markets of the east coast. The population rose from 31.4 to 76.2 million between 1860 and 1900. This created a massive demand for goods and the economy boomed.

Despite a divisive civil war between the industrial North and the agricultural South in the 1860s, as the 20th century approached, the USA was poised to become the world's industrial leader.

How the railways powered industrialization

Once the railway network had been largely completed in Britain, navvies and contractors took their expertise and built railways all over the world. One of the most successful British contractors was Thomas Brassey, who was responsible for railway lines in Canada, France, the Crimea (Russia), Australia, Argentina and India.

The historic moment when the USA's east and west coasts were connected by the railroad. Celebrations were held at Promontory Summit, Utah on 10 May 1869.

The countries that wanted to industrialize understood the importance of railway building and learned from the British experience. They realized that railways created a service and a market for the economy. On the service side, railways were a quicker and cheaper method of transport than either roads or canals. If costs were low, goods were cheaper and this increased demand. Factory owners and producers saw a railway link as highly desirable. They could bring in raw materials and dispatch their finished products cheaply. Passenger travel allowed the workforce to be more mobile and flexible.

The construction of a railway network acted as a huge market for the products of the industrial revolution. Vast amounts of iron were required for track, steam locomotives, tools, supplies and spare parts to keep the railways running. Iron and timber were needed in large quantities for bridges and the often immense viaducts that were being built. When the boom in German railway building took place in the 1840s, it gave a great boost to the iron, machine-building and coal industries.

In the USA, the first transcontinental railway was completed in 1869, when the United Pacific

Railroad, coming from the west, met the Central Pacific Railroad coming from the east at Promontory Summit in Utah. The directors of both companies hammered in a golden spike on which was written the words *'May god continue the unity of our country as this Railroad unites the two great oceans of the world'*. This was a sincere desire in the aftermath of a destructive civil war. Railways could bring a country closer together, just as the German rail network had helped bind together the states of the German confederation. In large countries such as Russia, Canada and the USA, the railway could help governments keep control of outlying areas.

Above all, railways allowed business to develop. In the USA, when the railroad reached the cattle towns of Abilene, Dodge City and Wichita, Chicago developed the biggest slaughtering and meat-packing industry in the world. Longhorns (a breed of cow) from Texas were driven up the cattle trails for $4 a head. When they reached Chicago by train they were sold for $40 each.

In all the industrializing nations, the railway had a huge effect on urbanization. Once railway lines radiated out from the centre of a city, builders bought up land and built streets of houses. Stations serving these suburbs were opened, and workers could commute to jobs in the city centres.

POSTER

The Union Pacific Railroad tried to attract a whole range of passengers to cross the continent in their trains.

33

Steamships and world trade

With many countries producing more goods in the period after 1840, there was a tenfold increase in the total volume of world trade. This was assisted by the construction of large iron steamers that carried cargoes around the world's numerous shipping lanes.

Although the first steamship to cross the Atlantic was the US steamer *Savannah* in 1819, it ran out of coal before reaching Ireland (sails then had to be used to complete the journey). In April 1838 the possibilities of ocean-going steam travel became clear. The great civil engineer Isambard Kingdom Brunel designed a paddle steamer (a ship powered by steam and paddle wheels), *The Great Western*, which sailed from Bristol to the USA in 15 days and 15 hours. The quickest sailing ships before this were the clippers that could make the fastest crossing in 35 days.

Paddle steamer wheels were fragile and could be damaged at sea. In July 1843 Brunel launched the *SS Great Britain*, an all-iron ship that was driven by propellers. In 1845 it crossed the Atlantic in 14 days and 21 hours.

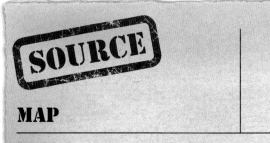

MAP

This is a French map drawn in 1912 showing the main world trade routes. Steamships allowed vast quantities of goods to be traded around the globe.

As well as the development of faster steamships, the first Atlantic cable linking Europe and the USA was completed in 1866 (with the help of another Brunel ship, the *SS Great Eastern*), which also helped in the expansion of trade. In 1869, the Suez Canal was opened, which cut the voyage times between Europe and the Far East. The world was becoming smaller and smaller as travel and communications improved.

Britain became the world's leading sea-trading nation. By 1913, nearly half of the world's steamships were British and one half of all the world's seaborne trade was carried in imported British ships.

At this time, Britain was a great supporter of the idea of 'free trade'. This was the belief that all nations should be able to trade with each other without taxes known as tariffs. These were taxes on imports coming into a country and made the goods more expensive. Britain disliked tariffs because it felt they restricted and lessened general prosperity. Free trade obviously suited Britain when it was the only industrial power because it wanted to sell as many goods abroad as possible. The emerging industrial powers such as Germany and the USA wanted to protect their new industries, so they put tariffs on imports as a defence against British goods.

The world's industrial powers had to constantly search for new customers and markets. They tried to find new markets, for example in South America, China and the Far East, where they could sell their goods. Trade could also occur in the other direction. Refrigerator ships carried cheap meat from Australia, New Zealand and Argentina to Europe. Australia also exported wool, which kept the British and German woollen mills well supplied.

The port of Hamburg was known as Germany's 'gateway to the world'. It was founded in the 12th century and became central Europe's most important port in the Industrial Revolution.

Many countries as well as Britain built up empires around the globe. Belgium, France, Portugal and Germany all had colonies by 1914. The colonies became ready-made markets for the mother country's exports. For example, most Lancashire cotton was exported to clothe the inhabitants of India. This occurred even though India had produced the world's finest cotton yarn and textiles until the 18th century.

The importance of cities

One of the most important results of industrialization and population increase was the growth of cities – urbanization. As agriculture modernized, hundreds and thousands of people from the rural areas in Europe could no longer find a livelihood in the countryside. They had to try to find work in the cities instead.

A bird's-eye view of Birmingham, England, in 1860. The city, with the arrival of the canal system, became one of the most important manufacturing centres in the country.

Not surprisingly, the areas that grew quickest were the settlements with factories. In Britain between 1801 and 1851, Birmingham saw its population rise from 73,000 to 250,000. The population of Liverpool, the port that imported cotton from the USA, increased from 77,000 to 250,000. Manchester in 1772 had 25,000 inhabitants; by 1851 it had 368,000. Similar increases happened in France

and Germany. Moscow in Russia had a population of 400,000 by the late 19th century. One by one, countries had more urban than rural dwellers: Britain in 1851, Germany by 1900 and the USA by 1920.

Industrial cities were noisy and dirty. However, there were attractions. They offered jobs, much higher wages than those in the countryside and shops full of a variety of goods. Cities had colourful markets, entertainment in music halls and theatres, and company to be found in pubs, taverns, bars and dance halls. The average age of city

SONG

'This Manchester's a fine place,
For trade and other such like movements;
What town can keep up such a race,
As ours has done for prime improvements;

For of late what sights of alterations,
Both streets and buildings changing stations,
Cry bout, "Laws! Pickle and preserve us!"
Sing hey, sing ho, sing hey down, gaily,
Manchester's improving daily.'

Broadside ballad, written between 1830 and 1850.
Quoted in *Nature and Industrialization*, ed Aladair Clayre.

dwellers was lower than that in the countryside. Inhabitants in the cities had an average age of between 20 and 40.

Culturally, the cities were much richer than in the countryside. There were parks, libraries, Mechanics Institutes (offering evening classes), and daily, morning and evening newspapers. It was the age of exhibitions. The first was in London in 1851; it was called The Great Exhibition and took place in Hyde Park. Paris, France followed suit in 1855, Philadelphia, USA in 1876, Chicago, USA in 1893 and Turin, Italy in 1896. For many people, the cities were places of opportunity and improvement.

Not only did cities act as magnets for people in the surrounding countryside, but they also attracted migrants from further afield. For example, many people, desperate to better themselves, travelled from other countries to reach Paris or Berlin.

There were similar migrations to other cities. Belgians and Germans helped develop the French towns of Roubaix and Mulhouse. Poles sought work in the heavy industrial centre of the Ruhr in Germany. Irish labourers flocked to British cities, especially Liverpool and Glasgow.

The poorest passengers take the air on the decks of the **SS Pennland,** *an emigration ship that sailed the Atlantic from Europe to the USA in the late 19th century.*

Throughout the 19th century the USA offered great opportunities and was very attractive to European populations. Risking everything on dangerous Atlantic crossings on the notorious 'coffin ships', (so called because many died) millions migrated to the USA looking for a better life.

In the late 19th century, the largest city in the USA was New York. It was the first port of call for immigrants and had a population of more than 1.5 million in 1890. The majority of them were born in Europe: 211,000 from Germany, 190,000 from Ireland, 49,000 from Russia, 48,000 from Austro-Hungary, 40,000 from Italy and 36,000 from England.

Conditions in the cities

The huge flood of migrants into the industrial towns and cities for work caused overcrowding and placed serious strains on the undeveloped infrastructure. In British cities such as Manchester, it was impossible for builders to keep up with the increase in people. Old houses were crammed full of families who had to live in one room or even share it with another family. The city's basements were notoriously bad to live in. When it rained they filled up with filthy water.

Any new working-class housing was hastily and poorly built, damp, unhygienic and lacked ventilation. In these conditions, diseases spread easily. In 1837, the year Queen Victoria came to the throne, 59,000 people died of the highly infectious lung disease tuberculosis. This disease was common throughout Europe and the USA.

Working-class people were housed in the cheaper districts and had to live among the unpleasant trades that involved the killing and processing of animals for their meat. Workers in slaughterhouses and leather tanneries threw animal waste into drains or streams, or left them to rot. The smells, flies and filth were shocking. The most serious threat to these crowded cities came from the lack of sanitation. The expanding cities had no proper sewers.

Human sewage was deposited in cesspits (holes in the ground that overflowed with rain water), drains, dumps, streams and rivers. This sewage infected the drinking water and caused the killer disease cholera. Europe was hit by serious cholera outbreaks in 1831-2, 1848-9 and in 1866-7.

As well as disease, fire and crime were constant threats. On 8 October 1871 a fire broke out in Chicago destroying 17,500 buildings and causing $200,000,000 of damage. Three hundred people were killed and 90,000 were made homeless. Crime rates in the industrial cities were high. Many cities had areas that

SOURCE

REPORT

'Punderson's Gardens, Bethnal Green, London. Along the centre of the street is an open, sunk gutter, in which, filth of every kind is allowed to accumulate and putrefy … in wet weather, the gutter overflows; its contents are poured into neighbouring houses …'

Dr Southwood Smith explained the hazards of east London life in the *4th Report of the Poor Law Commissioners* in 1838.

were dangerous and unsafe. New York had its notorious slum area called 'Five Points' and London had St. Giles 'Rookery'. Both areas were populated by pickpockets, murderers and illegal gamblers. There were major disturbances by gangs in New York. During 1834–44 there were 200 riots.

During times of unrest in early 19th-century Paris, protesters used to block

SOURCE

CARTOON

This is a sketch called *Doing the Slums*. It shows a policeman in the violent Five Points area in New York.

the narrow streets to prevent police and soldiers from entering. In the 1860s, these streets were demolished and replaced by elegant boulevards that were wide enough for troops to march down.

The overcrowded cities contributed to the class divisions of the 19th century. The rich fled the city centres and lived

separately from the working class. Police forces were introduced by most cities. The London Peelers was formed in 1829. Ordinary people disliked these forces at first because they seemed to be on the side of the rich city dwellers. In time, however, they became familiar and were generally accepted by most.

How things improved

All the countries that went through the transformation from a rural to an urban economy experienced difficult times. There is no doubt that the early years of industrialization caused severe hardship for many people. However, in time, governments did respond to these difficult challenges and progress – albeit slow in many cases – was made.

In Britain, there was major concern about the exploitation of many workers, especially children in the mines and factories. Long campaigns for reform did eventually bear fruit. The Mines Act of 1842 prohibited women and children under ten from working underground. In 1847, after

16 years of campaigning, the Ten Hours Act was passed, which limited women and children under 18 to working 58 hours a week. In 1850 and 1853 this law had to be tightened to

SOURCE

MAP

This map shows Bazalgette's plan for the main sewer lines, which were constructed in 1865 to improve the sewage system of London.

Metropolitan Board of Works.
MAP
Showing the Lines of
MAIN INTERCEPTING SEWERS,
CONSTRUCTED FOR THE IMPROVED DRAINAGE OF
THE METROPOLIS,
and the Purification of the
RIVER THAMES,
1865.
J. W. BAZALGETTE, ENGINEER

stop shifts going over ten hours. This legislation only protected children in factories. For the thousands of children under ten working in workshops and sweatshops, protection did not come until 1878. These laws were enforced by a few inspectors.

Gradually, cities were cleaned up. After the 'big stink' of the summer of 1859, when the River Thames overflowed with human sewage, the government decided to act. Joseph Bazalgette designed and built an impressive 81-mile underground sewage system for London that used steam engines pumping clean water to wash the sewage away through glazed pipes. This type of system was applied widely throughout Europe and the USA. Over time, the birth rate began overtaking the death rate in many European cities.

Parks were created and cities became more pleasant. In Paris, the authorities removed ancient cemeteries and put landscaped parks in their place. Streets were widened and paved and lit by gaslight. They were patrolled by police to make them safer. The unacceptable slum areas in many cities were slowly bought up and cleared. In Britain, the Artisans Dwelling Act empowered local authorities to carry this out.

The idea of holidays developed, ranging from cheap day trips to fortnights at fashionable resorts. People became more mobile and late

trains ensured that people could visit theatres or music halls and return to the suburbs before midnight.

Schools were set up in all the industrialized countries, and literacy rates rose steadily. With an educated workforce it was believed that a country would be more industrially competitive. This in turn gave rise to daily newspapers, an idea pioneered in the USA by Joseph Pulitzer and William Randolph Hearst and copied throughout Europe. A new age of communications was dawning when Alexander Graham Bell, a Scotsman, demonstrated his telephone in 1876.

As traffic jams increased, many cities followed London's lead and created an underground railway system. The Paris Metro, which opened in 1900, has some distinctive station entrances like this one.

Social problems

Although the Industrial Revolution achieved amazing progress in a relatively short space of time, there is no doubt it created winners and losers. In 1900 many European and Americans were better paid, clothed, fed, educated and had more free time than their grandparents. However, there was a large minority of people who did not share in the developing prosperity.

The alleged leader of the Luddites 'drawn from life' by an army officer in 1812. Note the burning mill in the background. Rioters blackened their faces or even dressed as women in an effort to conceal their identities.

From its early days, the Industrial Revolution had its casualties and critics. In Britain, skilled manual workers were suspicious of new machines that might put them out of work. In 1811 during the Luddite riots, centred on Nottinghamshire, rioters attacked the wide stocking frames that produced stockings called 'cut-ups' more quickly – but of inferior quality. Popular stories told of a leader called Ned or General Lud, organizing groups of well-disciplined men and leading them to target a particular village and destroy the frames and burn any cut-ups. Inspired by the Luddites, hand-loom weavers in Lancashire and Cheshire attacked the new power looms that were being installed. The government responded by introducing the death penalty as the punishment for machine breaking.

There was a similar leader in the countryside called Captain Swing, he appeared during 1830–1. Farm labourers attacked new threshing machines that deprived them of their winter work in the barns threshing by hand. Nineteen of these rioting farm labourers were hanged and hundreds transported to Australia.

The Chartist Movement of the 1830s and 1840s tried to bring working people into the political world with a list of demands called the People's Charter, which included universal suffrage and annual parliaments. The charter failed because it scared off many of the wealthier supporters; the Chartists' energies then went into trade unions, which at first represented only the better-paid and more skilled workers.

The publication in the USA of Henry George's *Progress and Poverty* (1879) was widely read on both sides of the Atlantic. It questioned why, when nations were becoming richer, the poor seemed to be so numerous. George himself suggested that a tax on land owners might counter inequality.

Workers in the USA found it difficult to improve their pay and conditions. If trade unionists went on strike, employers responded with lockouts. This meant all employees, even those not striking, were stopped from work. They brought in strike-breakers (workers to do the strikers' jobs) and sometimes brought in the army. During a strike at the Pullman Railway Factory in 1894, President Grover Cleveland sent in the troops to call an end to the strike. The American

REPORT

'Man is the only animal whose desires increase as they are fed; the only animal that is never satisfied.'

Henry George (in the picture below) tried to account for the huge division between rich and poor in *Progress and Poverty*, 1879.

Railway Union was destroyed. Large unions that were formed for both skilled and unskilled workers such as the Knights of Labour (1869) and the American Federation of Labour all failed. They suffered from the widely held view that somehow trade unions were 'un-American'.

Poverty and the legacy of the Industrial Revolution

By the late 19th century there was a growing unease in Britain and the USA that a significant number of people were living on or below the poverty line. In 1890, Jacob A. Riis published *How the Other Half Lives*, a shocking description of slum life in New York. Charles Booth and Seebohm Rowntree both discovered that between a quarter and a third of people living in the British cities of London and York lived in severe poverty.

Industrialization brought about the problem of the exploitation of child labour. These boys worked the night shift in a glassworks in Indiana, USA in 1908. Such exploitation still occurs today.

This may have been because 19th–century governments had chosen not to involve themselves directly in the affairs of private business, the economy or social problems unless absolutely necessary. The strength of non-interventionist or laissez-faire ideas slowly became less popular. In Germany, the government set up compulsory insurance schemes for worker illness (1883) and accident disability (1884).

In Britain after 1834, a poor person who wanted relief would have to enter a workhouse. Workhouses were deliberately made unpleasant to deter people from applying for help. In practice, they contained the weakest and most vulnerable members of society, such as orphans or the elderly. The new Liberal government elected in 1906 tried to do something for the UK's poorest people. The government passed laws that set up Old Age Pensions (1908) and National Insurance schemes for unemployment and sickness (1911).

Obviously the story of the Industrial Revolution does not end here. Industrialization, with its successes and failures, continues today. The high standard of living that the developed world enjoys can be directly traced to the Industrial Revolution. Its legacy has left us with some major challenges: our reliance on unsustainable fossil fuels; over-consumption; pollution of the planet; the lack of fair trade for developing countries and the dreadful poverty these countries experience.

44

TIMELINE

1694	The Bank of England is founded.
1709	Abraham Darby uses coke to smelt iron ore instead of charcoal.
1712	Newcomen engine pumps out a coal mine in Birmingham, England.
1733	John Kay's Flying Shuttle weaves cloth more quickly than ever before.
1751	184 Turnpike Trusts established to improve the road network.
1761	Bridgewater Canal opens.
1769	Watt develops his separate condenser, making Newcomen engines more efficient.
1776	Adam Smith's *The Wealth of Nations* is published.
1777	The Grand Trunk Canal, linking the rivers Trent and Mersey, opens.
1779	Crompton's Mule combines all the strengths of the Spinning Jenny and the Water Frame.
	World's first iron bridge spans the River Severn at Coalbrookdale, England.
1781	Watt develops his rotary motion steam engine.
1784	Cort develops puddling and rolling techniques for producing wrought iron.
1787	John Wilkinson builds the world's first iron barge.
1789	Samuel Slater emigrates from England to the USA and transforms the textile industry.

1793	Eli Whitney develops his cotton gin in the USA.
	Robert Fulton begins work on his paddle steamer.
1800	Eli Whitney develops rifle construction with interchangeable parts.
1805	Richard Trevithick's steam locomotive Catch Me Who Can on show in London.
1807	Robert Fulton's paddle steamer *Clermont* operates on the Hudson River, New York.
1825	The Erie Canal opens in the USA.
	The Stockton to Darlington Railway opens with George Stephenson's Locomotion.
1830	The Liverpool to Manchester Railway opens with George and Robert Stephenson's Rocket.
1838	Brunel's steamship the *Great Western* crosses the Atlantic from London to New York.
1840–51	Railway Mania in Britain. 7,000 miles of track completed by 1851.
1845	Brunel's *SS Great Britain*, the world's first iron ship driven by propellers, crosses the Atlantic.
1863	World's first underground railway opens in London.
1866	Joseph Bazalgette's underground sewage system in London completed.
1869	USA's first transcontinental railway completed.

GLOSSARY

Apprentice
Someone who is legally bound to an employer while he or she learns a trade.

Aqueduct
A man-made channel carrying water over a river valley.

Assembly
To fit or put something together in an industrial process.

Blast furnace
A very hot area for smelting metals.

Bobbins
Wooden cylinders for winding thread.

Boom
A period of economic prosperity and growth.

Cheque
A written order to a bank to pay out money.

Civil engineer
An engineer who builds bridges, roads, canals, tunnels and railways.

Colliery
Coal mine and the buildings linked to it.

Colony
Country or area ruled by another country.

Commute
To travel some distance from home to a place of work.

Conurbation
A large built-up area consisting of a number of towns that are close together.

Deposits
Amounts of a metal or mineral that has built up naturally in the ground over time.

Domestic system
System of industry that took place at home.

Empire
A geographical area that is owned and controlled by a particular country.

Entrepreneur
A person who organizes business and commercial projects that contain financial risk.

Forge
A workshop that smelts and shapes metal.

Foundry
Building for casting or shaping metal.

Heavy industry
Large-scale industry producing metal and machines.

Infrastructure
The basic foundations of a city, such as roads, sewers, transport links and street lighting.

Laissez-faire
From the French 'leave be' or 'leave alone,' the view that governments should not interfere with business.

Locks
A section of a canal with gates at each end letting water in and out. Locks allow barges to go up and down hills.

Loom
A frame for weaving cloth.

Manual
A job or task that is done by hand.

Millwright
A person who designs and builds textile mills.

Packhorse
A horse for carrying goods.

Paddle steamer
A ship that is propelled by paddle wheels at the side or rear of the hull.

Patent
An official document that protects an invention from being copied for a certain amount of time.

Pig iron
Smelted iron used for casting into objects.

Rural
In the countryside.

Sanitation
Keeping buildings and water supplies clean using drainage and the safe disposal of waste.

Seam (coal)
A layer of coal in the ground or in a mine.

Share
An investment of money in a company that entitles the owner to a share in the profits.

Smelt
To heat rock to extract the metal from it.

Sweatshop
A place of work with poor conditions, usually involving long hours and very low pay.

Synthetic dyestuffs
Artificially-made dyes used to colour objects.

Threshing
Hitting the ears of wheat to separate out the grain.

Trade unions
Organizations of workers. Through its leaders, the union could discuss better pay and conditions with the employer.

Transported
When criminals were sent as punishment to a colony in the USA or Australia.

Universal suffrage
When every adult can vote.

Urban
To do with a city or town.

Urbanization
The movement of people from rural to urban areas. The growth of towns and cities.

Workhouse
A place where people who could not look after themselves could go to live and work. Workhouses were often strict and unpleasant.

FURTHER INFORMATION

FURTHER READING

Empire and Industry 1700 –1900 by Ian Dawson, Oxford University Press, 2001

The Industrial Revolution – Events and Outcomes by Nigel Smith, Raintree, 2002

Witness to History: The Industrial Revolution by Sean Connolly, Heinemann Library, 2003

Life in Britain: Britain in the Industrial Revolution by Fiona Macdonald, Franklin Watts, 2007

WEBSITES

www.amberleymuseum.co.uk
Amberley Museum is dedicated to the industrial history of south-east England.

www.ironbridge.org.uk
Website about the iron bridge at Coalbrookdale.

www.sciencemuseum.org.uk
The website for the UK's Science Museum.

www.spartacus.schoolnet.co.uk/Industrial Revolution.htm
Site with large section on the Industrial Revolution.

PLACES TO VISIT

The Ironbridge Gorge Museum Trust
Coach Road, Coalbrookdale, Telford, TF8 7DQ

Museum of Science and Industry
Liverpool Road, Castlefield, Manchester, M3 4FP

The National Rail Museum
Leeman Road, York, YO26 WXJ

The North of England Open Air Museum
Beamish, County Durham, DH9 0RG

INDEX

Numbers in **bold** refer to illustrations.

Documenting History

Contents of titles in the series: